American Moments

ABDO
& Daughters

THE LOUISIANA PURCHASE

By Alan Pierce

VISIT US AT
WWW.ABDOPUB.COM

Published by ABDO Publishing Company, 4940 Viking Drive, Suite 622, Edina, Minnesota 55435. Copyright ©2004 by Abdo Consulting Group, Inc. International copyrights reserved in all countries. No part of this book may be reproduced in any form without written permission from the publisher.

Printed in the United States.

Edited by: Melanie A. Howard and Katharine Thorbeck
Contributing Editor: Tamara L. Britton
Interior Production and Design: Terry Dunham Incorporated
Cover Design: Mighty Media
Photos: Corbis, Library of Congress

Library of Congress Cataloging-in-Publication Data

Pierce, Alan, 1966-
    The Louisiana Purchase / Alan Pierce.
        p. cm. -- (American moments)
    Includes index.
    ISBN 1-59197-287-6
    1. Louisiana Purchase--Juvenile literature. [1. Louisiana Purchase.] I. Title. II. Series.

E333.P54 2004
    973.4'6--dc22

                                                                2003063878

CONTENTS

BENEFICIAL EVENT

On June 30, 1803, a stunning headline appeared in a Boston, Massachusetts, newspaper. The headline in the *Independent Chronicle* proclaimed, LOUISIANA CEDED TO THE UNITED STATES!

The story reported what is now known as the Louisiana Purchase. France had sold the vast Louisiana Territory to the United States. The vast area from the Mississippi River to the Rocky Mountains now belonged to the United States.

Most U.S. citizens were overjoyed as the news spread throughout the country. "It has the air of enchantment as the greatest and most beneficial event that has taken place since the Declaration of Independence," said Revolutionary War hero Horatio Gates about the purchase.

The Louisiana Purchase doubled the size of the nation, making it one of the largest countries in the world. Acquiring the territory also gave the United States control of the Mississippi River and the thriving port city of New Orleans.

But in 1803, no one knew Louisiana's exact borders and, consequently, no one knew the exact size of the territory. Europeans had not thoroughly explored the area. For more than 100 years, the

European kings who claimed Louisiana thought the territory was a wilderness of little value.

The Louisiana Purchase, however, would prove to be far from worthless for the United States. All or part of 15 states would be created from the territory.

But before any states could be created, the United States would first need to learn more about this mysterious land between the Mississippi River and the Rocky Mountains. In 1803, Americans knew almost nothing about the land their government had paid millions to buy.

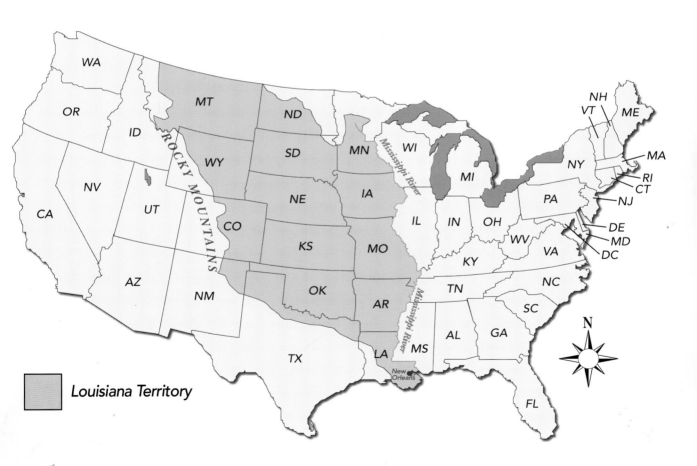

Louisiana Territory

SPAIN, FRANCE, AND LOUISIANA

The first Europeans to explore the interior of North America were Spanish. In 1521, Spain conquered the Aztec Empire in present-day Mexico. Spain then established a colony there, which was called New Spain. It produced a wealth of silver and gold for the Spanish treasury. From its colony, Spain sent out expeditions to seek more wealthy empires in North America.

A Spanish governor in Mexico named Francisco Vásquez de Coronado had heard stories about seven cities of gold called Cíbola. These rumors motivated Coronado to launch an expedition in 1540 into what is now the southwestern United States. Coronado's expedition encountered a pueblo of Zuni indigenous people.

Coronado and his men search for Cíbola.

The Zunis' stone and adobe village was clearly not the seven legendary cities of gold.

Coronado did not give up his dream of finding riches. In 1541, he searched for another wealthy city called Quivira. This expedition took him through land that would later be included in the Louisiana Purchase. He found a village of indigenous people near what is now Wichita, Kansas. But he never discovered any wealthy empires.

Another Spaniard named Hernando de Soto also searched for treasure in the continent's interior. In 1539, he sailed from Havana, Cuba, to present-day Florida. Stories about riches led De Soto through what are now the states of Georgia, the Carolinas, and Tennessee.

De Soto never found the wealth that prompted the expedition. But in 1541, his expedition reached the Mississippi River. The expedition crossed the river and stayed for the winter in present-day Arkansas. Later, De Soto fell ill with a fever and died

Hernando de Soto

in May 1542. De Soto's men buried him in the great river he had discovered for Spain.

Spaniards were not the only explorers to reach the Mississippi River. The French also explored it. Just as Spain had colonized Mexico, France had settled parts of present-day Canada. In the seventeenth century, French explorers followed the Great Lakes and the Mississippi River into the heart of North America.

An important French explorer was René-Robert Cavelier, Sieur de La Salle. La Salle saw the North American interior as an opportunity for wealth. But unlike the Spanish explorers, he was not interested in finding a fabulous city of gold. Instead, La Salle saw the Mississippi River and the Gulf of Mexico as potential areas for trade.

In 1682, La Salle traveled down the frozen Illinois River to the Mississippi River. After the ice cleared, La Salle and an expedition of Frenchmen and indigenous people canoed down the Mississippi. By April, the expedition had reached the part of the river near the Gulf of Mexico.

In early April, La Salle held an important ceremony. He claimed for France all the lands drained by the Mississippi River. No one, including La Salle, knew how much land this was. This area included all the land between the Alleghenies and the Rocky Mountains, and from the Gulf of Mexico to Canada. It totaled 1.2 million square miles, (3.1 million sq km) or six times the size of France in 1682.

La Salle named the immense territory Louisiana in honor of France's King Louis XIV. However, Louis XIV was not interested in the distant wilderness named after him. The French king was far more interested in his army in Europe and his new palace at Versailles.

René-Robert Cavelier, Sieur de La Salle

La Salle claims Louisiana for France.

The first French colonists finally arrived in Louisiana in 1699. France was fighting a war in Europe and did not adequately support the colonists. Settlements along the Gulf of Mexico in present-day Mississippi and Alabama struggled to survive.

Louisiana's first capital was in Mobile in modern-day Alabama. The French governor of Louisiana—Jean-Baptiste Le Moyne, Sieur de Bienville—decided to move the capital closer to the Mississippi River. A strategic location about 100 miles (161 km) upriver from the Gulf of Mexico was determined to be the best site for a capital city. In 1718, Bienville founded New Orleans, the new capital of the Louisiana Territory.

Louisiana and New Orleans failed to prosper in the eighteenth century. Part of the problem was that few new colonists settled in New Orleans. Disease and a sweltering climate deterred many French citizens from moving there.

French influence in other parts of the continent also weakened during this time. In 1754, France and England battled for control of North America in the French and Indian War. England captured the French stronghold of Quebec in Canada. With this defeat in 1759, France effectively lost control of Canada.

Before the war ended, France's King Louis XV decided to relinquish Louisiana. He offered Louisiana to Spain. Spain, which fought as France's ally in the war, had already lost Cuba and the Philippines to England. France presented Louisiana to Spain as compensation for land Spain had lost in the war.

Spain's King Charles III did not want to accept Louisiana, but he did so anyway. He thought Louisiana would at least provide a buffer between the growing English empire in North America and Spain's silver mines in Mexico. In 1762, the Treaty of Fontainebleau transferred New Orleans and the Louisiana Territory west of the Mississippi River to Spain.

The next year, the Treaty of Paris ended the French and Indian War. This treaty also marked the end of France's empire in North America. England gained Canada and all the French land between the Appalachian Mountains and the Mississippi River.

At first, the treaties of Fontainebleau and Paris had little impact on New Orleans and the colonists in Louisiana. The colonists believed for two years after the war that Louisiana was still French territory. Then in 1764, a letter from Louis XV informed the colonists that Spain now ruled Louisiana.

JEFFERSON LOOKS WEST

French kings had not been interested in Louisiana, but one man was intensely curious about the territory. That man was Thomas Jefferson. The library at his home in Monticello, Virginia, contained a large collection of books about western North America. Despite these books, very little was known about this part of the world. Rumors spread that woolly mammoths and unicorns roamed the continent's interior.

In 1783, Jefferson had more reason to be interested in the Louisiana Territory. That year, the Treaty of Paris had ended the Revolutionary War between the 13 American colonies and England. The United States was recognized as an independent country. In addition, the treaty extended the western border of the United States to the Mississippi River. Spain's Louisiana Territory was now a neighbor of the United States.

Thomas Jefferson

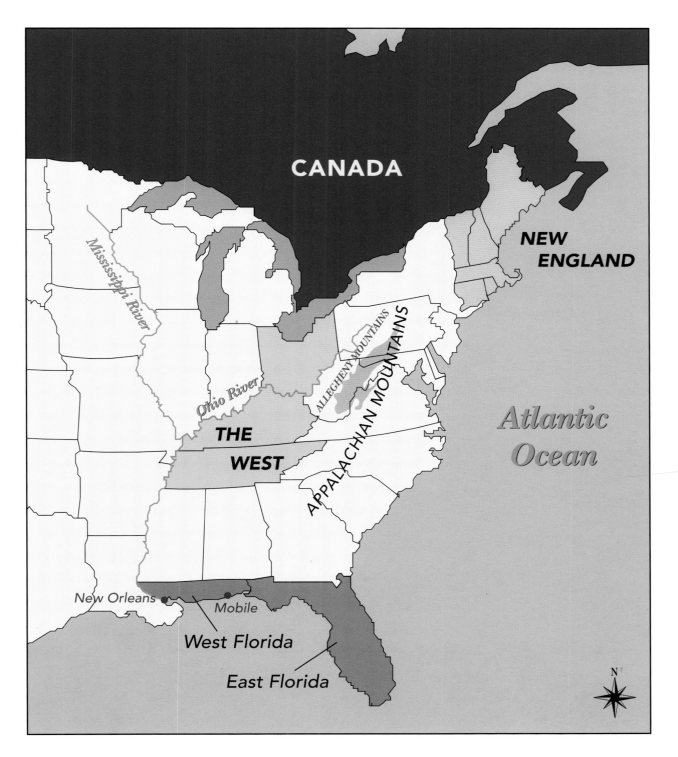

CANADA

NEW
ENGLAND

Mississippi River

Ohio River

ALLEGHENY MOUNTAINS

APPALACHIAN MOUNTAINS

THE

WEST

*Atlantic
Ocean*

New Orleans

Mobile

West Florida

East Florida

N

Jefferson had long been worried about a foreign power controlling the land west of the Mississippi River. Whoever ruled the interior of the continent could threaten the growth of the United States.

In 1784, Jefferson's fears became real. Spain closed the lower Mississippi River to foreigners, including Americans. Jefferson was serving as the U.S. minister to France, but he continued to follow events in the United States. Spain's act was a threat because thousands of Americans had migrated west to settle along the Mississippi and Ohio river valleys. The economic lives of these Americans depended on being able to navigate the Mississippi River and on having access to the port of New Orleans. Without access to New Orleans, these settlers could not transport their goods to oceangoing ships.

This crisis, however, was not just about a conflict between Spain and the United States. The crisis also revealed a split between Easterners and Westerners in the United States. At this time, the West was made up of the territories of Kentucky, Ohio, and Tennessee. Westward expansion had heightened tensions within the country. That tension was known as sectionalism.

Beginning in the late eighteenth century, different sections of the United States pursued distinct interests. New England states relied on shipbuilding, fishing, and international trade. Southern states used slaves to work plantations. Americans in the West wanted access to the Mississippi River and New Orleans.

These different interests led to tensions among sections of the country. For example, New Englanders opposed an expanding frontier. They wanted people to remain in the East to work in factories, stores, and banks. People in the future states of Kentucky

The Mississippi River valley

NEW ORLEANS

The French named New Orleans after Philippe II, the duke of Orléans. Philippe II governed France while the future king, Louis XV, was a boy. In 1721, New Orleans had a population of only 470 people. This included 193 slaves. Under Spanish rule, the city prospered as a trading port. By 1803, about 8,000 people lived in New Orleans.

The docks at port New Orleans

and Tennessee resented New England's attitude toward the frontier.

Meanwhile, the dispute about navigation on the Mississippi River continued. The United States attempted to solve the problem by appointing diplomat John Jay to negotiate a treaty. He negotiated with Spanish officials to arrive at a proposed treaty in 1786. The proposed treaty favored Easterners over Westerners. For example, the treaty would lower tariffs on American exports to Spain. This would benefit Eastern shippers. The treaty also would allow Spain to close navigation on the Mississippi for 20 or 30 years. This act would devastate Western farmers and shippers.

Jefferson criticized the proposed treaty. He believed navigation of the Mississippi River was vital for the entire country. Jefferson also feared that the treaty might cause Westerners to break away from the United States and form a separate country.

Ultimately, the debate over Jay's proposed treaty died down. Congress never ratified the treaty. Also,

Ships and boats crowd the water of the Mississippi River at New Orleans. New Orleans grew to prominence as the port at the mouth of the river.

American trade on the Mississippi River did not stop. Shippers were still able to smuggle goods through New Orleans.

Western trade on the Mississippi River later received a boost. In 1795, U.S. diplomat Thomas Pickney negotiated a treaty with Spain. It guaranteed the United States navigation rights on the lower Mississippi River. The treaty also allowed American shippers to store their goods in New Orleans without having to pay duties, or taxes.

Residents in Kentucky cheered the treaty. And they had good reason to celebrate. By 1798, the new states of Kentucky and Tennessee—along with the Indiana, Ohio, and Mississippi territories—shipped $3 million in goods to New Orleans.

NAPOLÉON'S EMPIRE

Events that would have a big impact on Louisiana were also occurring in France. The most significant was Napoléon Bonaparte's rise to power. Napoléon first rose to prominence as an army officer during the French Revolution. In 1799, Napoléon toppled the revolutionary government that had replaced the monarchy. Napoléon's official title was first consul, but in reality he ruled France as a dictator.

Napoléon was an ambitious man who planned to make France the greatest power in the world. As part of his plan, he wanted to regain France's territory in North America. Instead of turning to war, Napoléon used diplomacy to regain Louisiana from Spain. In 1800, French officials began negotiating with Spain's King Charles IV and Queen Maria Luisa.

It turned out that Napoléon had willing partners for the negotiation. Spanish first minister Manuel de Godoy wanted to get rid of Louisiana. The territory cost Spain a large amount of money to administer, and, unlike Mexico, Louisiana did not produce much revenue for Spain. Also, most of the colonists in Louisiana continued to speak French.

Napoléon made his offer to the Spanish king and queen. He would give them land in northern Italy, and in exchange, France would get

Napoléon Bonaparte

NAPOLÉON BONAPARTE

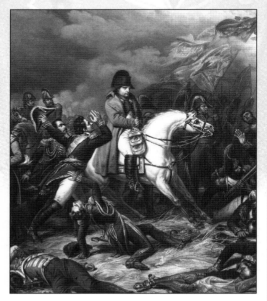

After selling the Louisiana Territory, Napoléon declared himself emperor of France. By 1807, Napoléon ruled most of the European continent, although Britain continued to oppose him. In 1815, British and Prussian forces defeated Napoléon at the Battle of Waterloo. The British later exiled Napoléon to the tiny island of St. Helena in the southern Atlantic Ocean. He died there in 1821.

Napoléon at Battle of Waterloo

Louisiana. The land in Italy would be called the Kingdom of Etruria. The king and queen's daughter, Luisetta, and her husband, Luis, would be allowed to rule the kingdom. King Charles and Queen Maria Luisa eagerly accepted the deal.

In October 1800, Spain and France signed the Treaty of San Ildefonso. This secret agreement gave Louisiana to France. Napoléon also gave his word that France would never give Louisiana to any other country but Spain. Napoléon wanted to keep the treaty a secret because he did not want the United States or Britain to attack Louisiana before French troops could arrive in North America.

The treaty, however, failed to settle the issue of the Floridas. At that time, Florida was divided into two provinces, West Florida and East Florida. East Florida included the present-day state of Florida. West Florida included a strip of land along the Gulf of Mexico that encompassed parts of the present-day states of Louisiana, Mississippi, and Alabama.

France and Spain did not agree on whether West Florida was part of the Louisiana Territory.

Meanwhile, Napoléon planned the French occupation of Louisiana. But he faced a serious problem. Napoléon wanted to use the island of St. Domingue in the Caribbean Sea as a base to send troops and supplies to Louisiana. St. Domingue, now called Haiti, had been a French colony. But in 1791, slaves on the island had revolted. France lost control of the island. Toussaint L'Ouverture, the revolt's leader, ruled St. Domingue.

Napoléon was determined to take back the island. In December 1801, France launched a fleet with thousands of soldiers to invade St. Domingue. Napoléon did not lead the attack. Instead, his brother-in-law general Charles Leclerc commanded the invasion.

The French expected an easy victory over people who had recently been slaves and had no formal military training. The invasion, however, was a complete disaster for the French. The slaves turned out to be effective fighters. Yellow fever also claimed the lives of many French soldiers. In September 1802, Leclerc informed Napoléon that the French had lost thousands of men and more troops would be needed to subdue the island. Napoléon's dream of restoring France's glory in North America had turned into one of his most costly mistakes.

Charles Leclerc

21

THE NOBLEST WORK

Just as conditions had changed in Europe and Louisiana, so, too, had the situation changed in the United States. Jefferson had won the presidency in 1800. An enthusiastic and longtime supporter of Western Americans now occupied the White House.

Jefferson soon faced a potential crisis. Rumors about France's acquisition of Louisiana had reached the U.S. government, despite the secrecy of the Treaty of San Ildefonso. France's possible ownership of Louisiana was troubling news. Jefferson did not want to see territory bordering the United States become part of Napoléon's empire. The United States viewed Spain as a weak country. But France was a powerful nation with a mighty army. It also had an ambitious ruler with plans to win back the land it had lost in North America.

In response to France's possible acquisition of Louisiana, U.S. secretary of state James Madison gave instructions to Robert Livingston, the U.S. minister to France. Livingston's task was to inquire about purchasing West Florida from France. West Florida referred to New Orleans. U.S. diplomats, however, could not get definite answers from France or Spain about which country owned West Florida.

In March 1801, the U.S. minister to England, Rufus King, had confirmed that France had gained possession of Louisiana. In an 1802 letter to Livingston, Jefferson warned that the United States would not tolerate French control of New Orleans. The president threatened that the United States would form an alliance with Britain to oppose France.

As the U.S. minister to France, it was Livingston's job to present this tough message to Napoléon's government. Livingston, however, chose to persuade French officials that occupying Louisiana was more trouble than it was worth.

Another idea emerged during Jefferson's discussions with his friend Pierre Samuel Du Pont de Nemours. Jefferson had met Du Pont while serving as the U.S. minister to France. Du Pont had escaped to the United States during the French Revolution. In the Spring of 1802, Du Pont was planning to return to France. Jefferson asked to talk to him about Louisiana.

The president discussed with Du Pont the possibility of fighting France to capture New Orleans. Du Pont, however, suggested buying New Orleans. Purchasing the land would be cheaper than a war, and no one would die.

When Du Pont arrived in France, he met with Napoléon. In the meeting, Du Pont proposed that France sell Louisiana as a way to

Robert Livingston

solve the crisis with the United States. Napoléon neither accepted the idea nor dismissed it.

While American and French leaders considered a peaceful solution, other events were driving the American people toward war. Newspapers in the United States reported that Louisiana now belonged to France. The American people were furious to learn that Napoléon's soldiers might soon be garrisoned on America's frontier.

Soon another event angered Americans even further. In the fall of 1802, a Spanish official named Juan Ventura Morales closed the New Orleans port to Americans. Apparently he believed the Americans were taking advantage of the Pickney Treaty and doing a lot of smuggling. Morales's action would have a devastating effect on American farmers and shippers. Instead of being shipped from the port, American goods would now rot before getting to market.

Most Americans suspected that Napoléon had given the order to close the port to U.S. shippers. The port's closing angered more than just Westerners. Americans throughout the country demanded war.

Jefferson responded to the public's call for war by nominating his friend James Monroe to serve in France with Livingston. The nomination in January 1803 was not solely a matter of friendship. For several years, Monroe had supported American navigation rights on the Mississippi River. This support made Monroe popular with Western Americans, and they trusted him to protect their interests. Livingston, on the other hand, was an Easterner from New York.

Monroe had the chance to help Western Americans in a significant way. He was going to France to buy New Orleans and the Floridas. Monroe was given the title of envoy extraordinary. This important-

James Monroe went on to serve as president of the United States from 1817 to 1825.

sounding title meant that Monroe had the power to act with the president's authority.

Monroe received more than titles before he went to France. He also received permission to spend money for the purchase. Congress approved spending $2 million to buy New Orleans and the Floridas. Jefferson, however, told Monroe that the United States could spend more than $9 million if the United States received a large part of the Floridas and navigation rights to the Mississippi River.

The discussion with Jefferson would not prepare Monroe for the situation in France. The scope of the negotiations had changed

THE LOUISIANA PURCHASE.
MESSRS. MONROE AND LIVINGSTONE COMPLETING NEGOTIATIONS WITH TALLYRAND, APRIL 30, 1803

Monroe and Livingston discuss the Louisiana Purchase with Talleyrand.

drastically. Napoléon now wanted to sell the entire Louisiana Territory to the United States.

Napoléon decided to sell Louisiana because his priorities had changed. France had lost thousands of soldiers in the failed attempt to capture St. Domingue. Without St. Domingue as a base, Napoléon abandoned his attempt to establish an empire in Louisiana. He now turned his attention to war with Britain.

Britain occupied Malta, a small but strategically important island in the Mediterranean Sea. Napoléon wanted to capture it for France. He knew a campaign against a powerful country such as Britain would require a large amount of money and resources.

Meanwhile, Livingston's negotiations with French officials were showing results. Since arriving in France, Livingston had discussed American interests with French foreign minister Charles Maurice de Talleyrand-Périgord and French finance minister François de Barbé-Marbois.

On April 11, 1803, Talleyrand asked Livingston if the United States would be interested in buying all of the Louisiana Territory. Livingston replied that the United States wanted only New Orleans and the Floridas. When Monroe arrived in Paris, Livingston informed him about Talleyrand's offer.

Two days later, Monroe and Livingston got another chance to buy all of the Louisiana Territory. This time, Marbois made another offer to Livingston. He offered the Louisiana Territory for a little less than $20 million. The two Americans were excited to learn about the prospect of buying the entire Louisiana Territory.

The Americans, however, faced a serious problem. Neither Monroe nor Livingston had the U.S. government's approval to buy the vast Louisiana Territory. Also, neither man had been allowed to spend the large sum of money France wanted for the land.

Monroe and Livingston's problem was made worse by the fact that they could not quickly consult Jefferson or Congress. In the days before telephone, telegraph, or e-mail, the only way to communicate across the Atlantic Ocean was by letter. In 1803, it might have taken a letter four to six weeks to travel from Paris to Washington DC. The Americans did not have that much time because Napoléon might change his mind.

Negotiations proceeded rapidly. By April 27, 1803, the Americans and French had reached an agreement. The United States would pay $15 million for Louisiana. Five days later, on May 2, Monroe and Livingston signed the Louisiana Purchase Treaty.

Not all of the $15 million would go to France, according to the treaty. In the 1790s, France had seized American ships and crews. The United States would use $3,750,000 to pay Americans who had been harmed by France's actions.

France received another benefit from the treaty. According to the treaty's terms, French and Spanish ships that used the New Orleans port would pay the same taxes as American ships using the port. This arrangement was to last for 12 years.

A huge question remained unanswered by the treaty. No one knew how much land the United States had bought for $15 million. The territory was understood to be the same territory that France had received from Spain in the Treaty of San Ildefonso. The true size of the territory would not be known until it was explored. Once known, the size of the Louisiana Purchase turned out to be about

828,000 square miles (2,144,520 sq km). The agreement meant the United States bought the land for about four cents per acre.

After signing the treaty, Livingston praised the negotiators' work. He said, "We have lived long but this is the noblest work of our whole lives. The treaty which we have just signed has not been obtained by art or dictated by force . . . It will change vast solitudes into flourishing districts. From this day the United States take their place among the powers of the first rank."

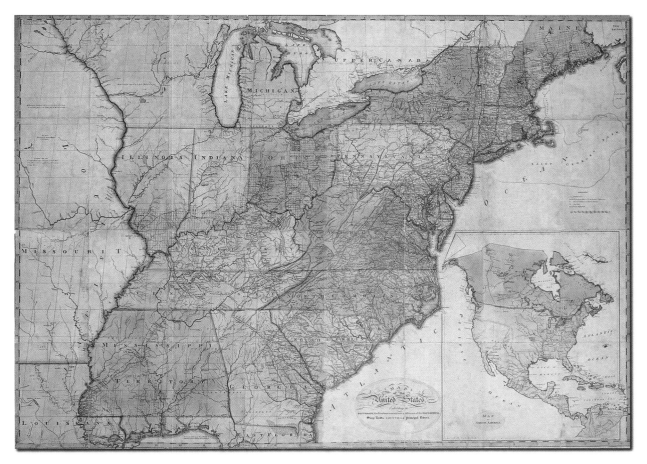

A map of U.S. territories and states east of the Mississippi River in 1804.

CONGRESS

Americans from all over the country were excited about the news of the Louisiana Purchase. Westerners hailed the expansion, and they joined Southerners in their admiration of Monroe. New Yorkers credited Livingston with securing the agreement.

Some U.S. leaders opposed the purchase. Members of the Federalist Party in Congress argued that the purchase was unconstitutional. They said the federal government could not acquire Louisiana unless each state approved the purchase. Opposition to the purchase was significant because the U.S. Senate still needed to ratify the Louisiana Purchase Treaty before the United States could accept the territory.

The most serious challenge to the purchase came from U.S. senator Timothy Pickering of Massachusetts. He was so angry that he planned a separate confederacy of northern states to break away from the United States. The plan to form a confederacy collapsed when efforts to get New York to join failed.

The Federalists were not the only ones who questioned the constitutionality of the Louisiana Purchase. The issue troubled Jefferson. The purchase violated his political principles. As an Anti-federalist, Jefferson believed in a strict interpretation of the Constitution. If the Constitution did not specifically give the federal government power to do something, then the government was forbidden to do it.

At one point, Jefferson considered writing an amendment to the Constitution that would allow the federal government to acquire territory. Madison, however, discouraged Jefferson from proposing an amendment. Passage of a constitutional amendment would take too much time and Napoléon could change his mind about the treaty.

Concerns about the constitutionality of the purchase failed to prevent the Louisiana Purchase Treaty from being ratified. On October 20, 1803, the Senate voted 24 to 7 to ratify the treaty. The U.S. House of Representatives, which had to authorize payment for the Louisiana Purchase, approved the treaty by a vote of 89 to 23.

THOMAS JEFFERSON

In 1804, Thomas Jefferson was reelected president of the United States. After serving his second term, Jefferson returned to his home in Monticello, Virginia. He later sold his collection of books to the government. This collection formed the basis of the Library of Congress. Jefferson also founded the University of Virginia in Charlottesville. He put his architectural talents to use by designing the buildings at the university.

Thomas Jefferson

U.S. TERRITORY

The second French rule of Louisiana had been brief. Louisiana's French prefect, Pierre Clément Laussat, had not arrived in New Orleans until March 1803. Laussat immediately had to contend with rumors that the United States was buying Louisiana. In August, the French government officially informed Laussat that the Americans had bought the territory.

On November 30, 1803, Spain formally transferred Louisiana to France. Spain had protested the fairness of the Louisiana Purchase Treaty. According to Spain's agreement with Napoléon, Louisiana was supposed to go back to Spain if France decided to give up the territory. However, Spain had only about 300 soldiers in the New Orleans area, and was too weak to oppose the United States.

The United States took possession of Louisiana on December 20, 1803. The new American governor of the Louisiana Territory, William C. C. Claiborne, and U.S. brigadier general James Wilkinson arrived in New Orleans with 500 troops.

The ceremony to transfer Louisiana to the United States took place at the Cabildo. This was the building where the Spanish governing council had met. An official read the treaty of transfer out loud. Laussat then presented Wilkinson with the keys to the city. Finally, Laussat, Wilkinson, and Claiborne signed the documents that transferred New Orleans and Louisiana to the United States.

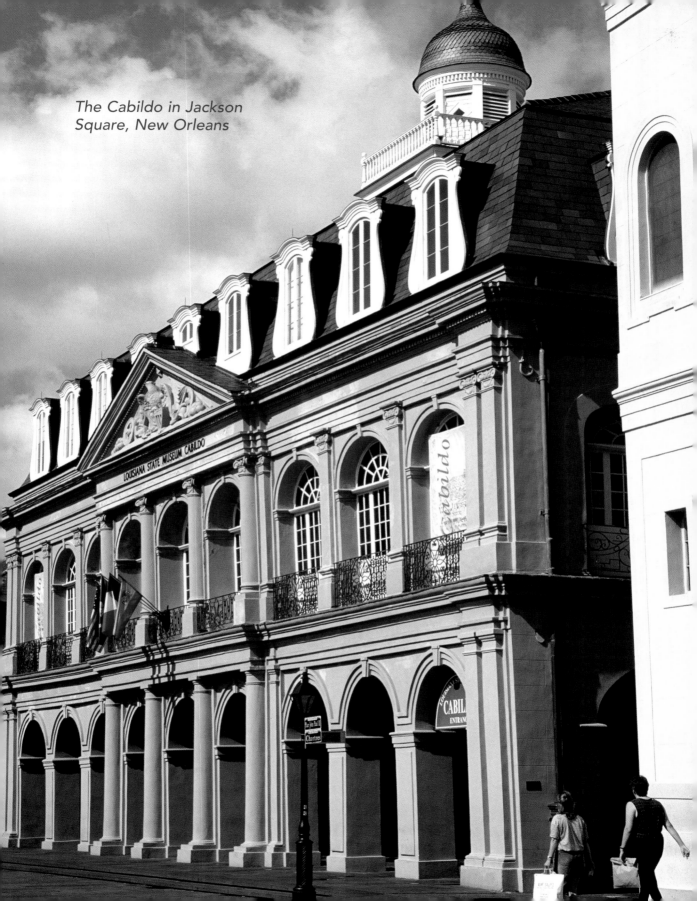

The Cabildo in Jackson Square, New Orleans

The three men walked onto the Cabildo's balcony to watch as the French flag was lowered and the American flag was raised. Soldiers fired their guns to honor the event. Claiborne reported that the city's residents welcomed the new American government.

In March 1804, another ceremony to mark the acquisition of Louisiana by the United States was held in St. Louis. Among those who attended the ceremony were Meriwether Lewis and William Clark. Lewis and Clark were about to embark on their famous exploration of the Louisiana Territory. The expedition was known as the Corps of Discovery.

The Corps had many goals. It planned to explore the Missouri River, look for a waterway to the Pacific Ocean, and study the new territory's plants and animals. In May 1804, Lewis, Clark, and about four dozen men set out in one keelboat and two small boats called pirogues to explore the Missouri River. They camped for the winter with Mandan and Hidatsa Native Americans near present-day Bismarck, North Dakota.

While staying with the Mandans and Hidatsas, Lewis and Clark met Sacagawea, a Shoshone woman. She proved to be a valuable translator as the expedition moved west to the Rocky Mountains.

In the spring, about a dozen men returned east with scientific specimens to give to Jefferson. A live prairie dog was among the specimens. In total, the expedition recorded 178 plants and 122 animals that had been previously unknown.

MERIWETHER LEWIS

Meriwether Lewis was born in Virginia on August 18, 1774. He was a gentleman farmer until 1794 when he joined militia volunteers and helped break up the Whiskey Rebellion. Later, when Thomas Jefferson asked him to lead the Louisiana Territory expedition, he trained with scientists from the American Philosophical Society so that he could make scientific reports.

WILLIAM CLARK

William Clark was born in Virginia on August 1, 1770. He served in the U.S. army from 1789 until 1796, when he resigned to work on his family's estate. Lewis chose Clark as his associate for the Louisiana Territory expedition. Clark was one of the first to document the Louisiana Territory. His maps of the territory and drawings of animals proved valuable to the expedition.

Sacagawea guides the Lewis and Clark expedition through the Rocky Mountains.

Lewis and Clark and the rest of the expedition continued over the Rocky Mountains, reaching the Pacific Ocean in November 1804. In March 1805, they began the long trek over the mountains back to St. Louis. They returned to St. Louis in September 1806.

Another development signaled America's control of the Louisiana Territory. In March 1804, Congress had divided the territory into two administrative parts. The southern part was named the Territory of Orleans. This territory included most of the present-day state of Louisiana. The northern part was known as the District of Louisiana. This vast District of Louisiana would later be divided into all or part of 14 states.

At first, the Indiana Territory was responsible for governing the District of Louisiana. But by 1805, the district had its own officials. In 1812, when Louisiana became a state, the District of Louisiana was renamed the Territory of Missouri.

The western border of the Louisiana Purchase was finally resolved with a treaty in 1819. The U.S. secretary of state, John Quincy Adams, and the Spanish minister to the United States, Luis de Onís y Gonzales, negotiated the treaty. In the treaty, the United States gave up claims to western territory that is now part of Colorado, New Mexico, Texas, and Wyoming. In return, Spain transferred Florida to the United States. Spain also withdrew its claims to the Oregon country, north of the present-day California border.

The Louisiana Purchase changed the way Americans thought about the country. Americans now accepted westward expansion across the continent as the country's purpose. Although the phrase Manifest Destiny wasn't used until the 1840s, the idea that the United States was meant to expand across the continent from the Atlantic Ocean to the Pacific Ocean would not have been conceivable without the Louisiana Purchase.

The Louisiana Purchase preceded many acts of territorial acquisition in the nineteenth century. Texas was annexed in 1845. In the Mexican War the United States seized California and the territory that now makes up the American southwest. This westward expansion, however, was also tragic for the Native Americans living between the Mississippi River and Rocky Mountains.

American Moments

CONSEQUENCES

Jefferson thought he knew what was best for Native Americans. He wanted to change their way of life. He believed that Native Americans who had survived by hunting should become farmers and live on less land. Later, the U.S. government adopted Jefferson's beliefs.

The Native Americans already living on the plains of the Louisiana Territory suffered greatly as American pioneers began to settle west of the Mississippi River. The pioneers brought with them diseases that killed thousands of the Native Americans. The pioneers' oxen and horses ate grass that fed the buffalo herds. Native Americans on the plains relied on the buffalo for their food. The number of buffaloes dropped, forcing Native Americans to fight each other for the chance to hunt fewer buffalo.

In 1851, the United States and major Native American tribes signed the Fort Laramie Treaty. The treaty confined tribes to certain sections of land. According to the treaty, the Native Americans had to stay on their allotted land. The United States would be allowed to build roads and military outposts within the Native Americans' lands. In exchange, the United States promised it would protect Native Americans from the pioneers.

The Louisiana Purchase caused another serious problem for the United States. The creation of more states from the Louisiana Territory inflamed the debate about slavery. Free states in the North did not want more slave states to join the Union, and slave states in

38

Plains Native Americans hunting buffalo

the South were worried about losing power if more free states were admitted. Both sides were concerned about whether free states or slave states would be created in the Louisiana Territory.

In 1817, the disagreement about slavery became critical when Missouri petitioned to enter the Union as a slave state. The debate led to the Missouri Compromise of 1820. The compromise allowed Missouri to enter the Union as a slave state and Maine to enter as a free state. In addition, the compromise banned slavery in the rest of the Louisiana Territory north of Missouri's southern border.

Although the Louisiana Purchase created troubles for the United States, it also brought about fantastic opportunities for the country. The natural resources within the states of the Louisiana Purchase have helped turn the United States into an economic leader.

At the time of the Missouri Compromise of 1820, the nation was divided between free states and territories and slave states and territories.

Free states and territories

Missouri Compromise Line

Slave states and territories

N

Steamboats load and unload cargo at the port of New Orleans.

Since the time of La Salle, people have recognized the potential of the Mississippi River. Today, 60 percent of the freight shipped on U.S. inland waterways travels down the Mississippi. Much of this freight is corn, soybeans, and wheat harvested from the rich soil of farm states.

The resources of the Louisiana Purchase are not limited to agriculture and rivers. Oklahoma is a leading oil producer. Wyoming mines more coal than any other state.

And yet, the significance of the Louisiana Purchase cannot be measured entirely by the value of its resources. Some have said the expanse of the land has helped create America's character. One hundred years after the Louisiana Purchase, President Theodore Roosevelt hailed its significance. He said the Louisiana Purchase "determined that we should be a great and expanding nation instead of relatively a small and stationary one."

TIMELINE

1540   Francisco Vásquez de Coronado leads an expedition into the North American interior.

1541   Hernando de Soto reaches the Mississippi River.

1682   René-Robert Cavelier, Sieur de La Salle, claims the Louisiana Territory for France.

1718   The French establish New Orleans.

1762   The Treaty of Fontainebleau transfers ownership of the Louisiana Territory from France to Spain.

1800   Spain returns the Louisiana Territory to France in the Treaty of San Ildefonso.

1802   In April, U.S. president Thomas Jefferson warns France not to occupy New Orleans.

1803   In April, U.S. diplomats Robert Livingston and James Monroe negotiate with France to buy the Louisiana Territory.

In May, U.S. and French officials sign the Louisiana Purchase Treaty.

In October, the U.S. Senate approves the Louisiana Purchase Treaty.

On December 20, the United States takes over possession of the Louisiana Territory.

1804 In March, Congress creates the Territory of Orleans and the District of Louisiana in the Louisiana Territory.

In May, Meriwether Lewis and William Clark lead an expedition of the Louisiana Territory and western North America.

1812 Louisiana becomes the first state created from the Louisiana Purchase to be admitted to the Union.

1819 The Adams-Onís Treaty establishes the western border of the Louisiana Purchase.

2003 States created from the Louisiana Territory celebrate the bicentennial of the Louisiana Purchase.

American Moments

FAST FACTS

The year 2003 marked the bicentennial of the Louisiana Purchase. Many celebrations in New Orleans and other parts of Louisiana marked this anniversary. For example, a re-enactment of the signing of the Louisiana Purchase Treaty took place at the Cabildo in December.

The U.S. Mint issued two special nickels in 2004 in honor of the Louisiana Purchase and Lewis and Clark expedition. The first nickel was issued in the spring. One side of the nickels displayed a handshake between a Native American and a U.S. military official. The fall coins featured a keelboat like the one that Lewis and Clark used to explore the Missouri River.

The Lewis and Clark expedition was not the only American attempt to explore the Louisiana Territory. William Dunbar, Zebulon Pike, and Thomas Freeman led different expeditions into the territory between 1804 and 1806.

James Monroe served as the fifth president of the United States from 1817 to 1825. He is famous for the Monroe Doctrine. It attempted to limit power of European nations in the Americas.

French settlers known as Cajuns contributed to Louisiana's culture. Cajuns originally settled in Canada. After the French and Indian War, the English expelled many Cajuns from Canada. Between 1765 and 1785, about 3,000 Cajuns arrived in Louisiana.

WEB SITES
WWW.ABDOPUB.COM

Would you like to learn more about the Louisiana Purchase? Please visit **www.abdopub.com** to find up-to-date Web site links about the Louisiana Purchase and other American moments. These links are routinely monitored and updated to provide the most current information available.

U.S. Captain Amos Stoddard accepts a document from Spanish officials at the transfer ceremony of the Louisiana Territory in St. Louis in 1804.

GLOSSARY

Anti-federalist: a politician in the late 1700s and early 1800s who opposed a strong national government and favored strict interpretation of the U.S. Constitution.

dictator: a ruler who has complete control and usually governs in a cruel or unfair way.

diplomat: a person who deals with representatives of other countries.

envoy extraordinary: a diplomat with less authority than an ambassador. An ambassador is a high ranking diplomat.

Federalist: a member of the Federalist Party. During the early 1800s, Federalists believed in a strong national government.

first consul: Napoléon Bonaparte's title in France. As first consul, Napoléon ruled as a dictator.

French Revolution: 1787 to 1799. A movement that led to the overthrow and execution of France's King Louis XVI. The monarchy was replaced by a succession of governments. The revolution ended when Napoléon Bonaparte seized control of the government.

indigenous: native.

Manifest Destiny: the belief that the United States' territorial expansion was divinely sanctioned.

negotiate: to settle an issue through discussion.

pirogue: a boat similar to a canoe.

prefect: a chief government officer.

relinquish: to give up or let go.

sectionalism: identification with a region of the United States.

yellow fever: a tropical disease transmitted by mosquitoes. Symptoms include headache, backache, fever, nausea, and vomiting. If patients do not recover, they can die within six to seven days of experiencing symptoms.

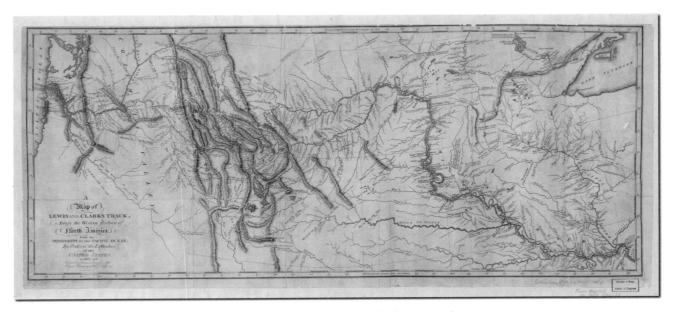

A map of the Lewis and Clark expedition

INDEX